Your Prosperity is Your Fault!

Activating your life's wealth streams

Dr. I. Franklin Perkins

dpRochelle
PO Box 9523
Hampton, Virginia 23670
dprochellepublishing.org

Your Prosperity is Your Fault!
Copyright © 2018
Dr. I. Franklin Perkins

Printed in the United States of America

Library of Congress – Catalogued in Publication Data

ISBN: 978-0-692-11253-3

First published by dpRochelle 4/28/18

Dedication

To anyone who is tired of lack!

Acknowledgments

Always thanks to my husband, son, and daughter for their support.

Thank You

Dr. Arnita Snead Brooks
Dr. Shirley Keech Clark
Tuesday Focus Group

Book Contents

WHY ME?

YES!!! Your Prosperity Is Your Fault!

If you are prospering or not prospering in life, it is your fault. You are totally responsible for the condition of your life or livelihood! Often, we blame others for the situations we encounter in life, but there is only one who can rightfully take the credit for whether you are triumphant or a failure and that one is. . . YOU!

There are various lectures, speeches, and commentaries written by powerful change agents about prosperity and the power to transform your life through positive thinking and speaking. So I am extremely grateful you have decided to read this material today. Aldous Huxley, a writer, novelist and philosopher states, "Every man who knows how to read has it in his power to magnify himself . . ." You have that magnifying opportunity at your fingertips right now!

For those of you who have been advocates for lifelong learning; perhaps, the information you will read in this book is not anything new nor is it an opportunity to "reinvent the wheel." If this is you, I beg your indulgence. But if this is your first time reading information like this, your life is getting ready to be radically changed. But regardless what "place" you come into this equation, this book was written to share another perspective regarding how natural laws congruently govern the level of prosperity we receive in life. It is my desire and hope also that if you did not activate these truths in the past that you would indeed do it after reading this book. When things are repeated, it is necessary to pay close attention, for your answer may lie within the echo. We learn by repetition.

As the old adage goes, "If you want something different you will need to do something different." To keep doing the same thing is pure insanity. So, if you like where you are in your life then put this book down now, before it inspires you to do something different!

Further, this information is designed to evolve your state of mind into a magnet

Everything on this earth

is designed to prosper you in

every area of your life.

for success and wealth as you have NOT lived your best life yet. There will be things cited that will revolutionize your thought process and possibly go against the grain of everything you have been taught about wealth. Allow it to make you so uneasy that it will ignite you to try to prove that it doesn't work . . . you will be surprised of your findings!

You should be aware that everything on this earth is designed to prosper you in every area of your life. But wait, I can hear you saying, "Didn't I hear somewhere that the poor will always be with us," YES, they will, but it does not say you have to be one of them. In reality, poor is a state of mind. You can be refined if you are insistent about your growth. You must CHANGE THE WAY YOU THINK about wealth, and the idea that you are not worthy of it. Your life is NOT destined for failure; neither do things have to stay the way that they are. YOU can have anything good that YOU desire if YOU can CHANGE YOUR MINDSET! Nothing should ever be "it is what it is," because YOU have the power to change whatever "it" is!

In these writings we will refer to a few laws that can activate the Universe to do for you what its name depicts. If you are familiar with metaphysics and other mind conditioning platitudes, you will be right at home. However, for those of you who are not, I will practically explain through short stories of actual accounts of the same. Anything that is considered a Law of the Universe will work regardless of who YOU are or where YOU are in life.

When we hear the word prosperity everyone tends to automatically think only about financial wealth. Yes, financial wealth is a part of prosperity; yet, not in totality. Here, the total package of prosperity is a lifestyle that requires the use of mental energy that will assist you in activating your wealth streams. This information gives you the power to change your current circumstances and can manifest whatever you desire. This includes love, joy, health, peace, a better life; and YES, financial wealth! After all, Henry David Thoreau, a 19th- Century essayist, philosopher and historian asserts, "Wealth is measured by the level of experience in all aspects of life."

Money does not make you better, it just makes you better off.

Therefore, a well-rounded life would have evidence of wealth. Soon after you learn how to operate your energy, you will be able to say, "Hello prosperity where have you been?"

Money is everywhere! It has not disappeared from the face of the earth nor has it taken wings to fly out of your reach to some faraway place. It is closer than you could ever imagine. The feelings and thoughts you have can either attract or repeal money. Of course, there is nothing wrong with YOU having some of it as an ancient writing declares that "money answers all concerns."

Please be aware that money does not make you better, *it just makes you better off.* I heard someone mention that more money reveals more of who you already are, whether that is good or evil. You will simply have more money to support whichever character you continuously nurture.

I've discovered that you don't have to wait until you are a billionaire to influence change for others, you can help them while you are on your way to new found wealth. Consequently, I chose not to wait for billionaire status to inform you of a better way. Since this is working for me, I have decided to teach anyone who will listen and show them how to open the pathway to their wealth streams and receive the great abundance that is available to all who actively disciplines themselves.

This book was initially written for the participants of my focus groups for a workable subject matter. Some of their declarations of good fortune are included in these writings as a proven success of accounts. They actively put these principles to practice and PRESTO, the windows and doors of opportunity began to overtake them, some within 24 hours, some within seven days and some over a few weeks!

You don't need to be religious for this to work for you. As a matter of fact, you don't need any religion at all for this to work for you because the Laws of the Universe do not discriminate.

In the upcoming chapters, we will rationally discuss: The Power of Your Mind, The Power of Your Words, The Power of

Your Imagination, The Power of Your Giving, The Power of Your Gratitude, The Power of Your Forgiveness, The Power of Your Love, and The Power of Your Putting It All Together as mastering each topic is vital to your success. You will find that obtaining

This Universe is rich and is designed to generate prosperous outcomes to anyone who desires to have it.

prosperity takes making a decision, focus, action, and great restraint. Once you discover how, it will transform your life from this day forward like never before.

If you are at the lowest point in your life, and have tried everything else, this is a great place to start by using these principles. The first thing you will need to do is change the way you think about prosperity. Don't ever let anyone make you feel guilty about wealth, or the desire to have more out of life. This Universe is rich and is designed to generate prosperous outcomes to anyone who desires to have it. If you do not desire better, then this manuscript will only serve you as a reminder of your possibilities and as a great read.

Let this information jump start and inspire you to a "call to action!"Don't try to copy the results, as you will have your own. Simply mimic the principles and document your outcomes, then you will understand why, 'Your Prosperity is Your Fault!'

THE POWER OF YOUR MIND

(Shifting Your Thoughts)

You possess the most potent weapon in the entire Universe!

Everybody wants a piece of it and many try to manipulate it or want to control it, but YOU are the only one who has the right to employ it; or YOU can choose to let someone else exploit it. If you haven't guessed by now . . . YES, I am talking about your MIND! This weapon of mass destruction is powerful and when used correctly, it can transform not only who you are but all things that concern YOU.

There is nothing new about mind power. It has resurfaced in different ways by various people who were in search of the truth of the mind. Unfortunately, many cannot comprehend the concept that their mind is strong enough to transform their entire life through their thoughts but it is not just a notion; it is TRUTH! Instead of receiving this truth some will deny that the power of the mind even exists. Perhaps, out of ignorance, yet they remain stuck in their sea of non-revelatory experiences. Denial is the thief of belief as it makes you consider that an intangible truth is not so. However, belief renders that there is an indiscernible greater truth than the apparent truth. Don't let this be YOU! Living in denial doesn't change the existence of truth. It will work one way or another whether you work it for your benefit or not.

What is the mind? Without getting wrapped up in a scientific discussion let me just tap on a few things. We are a three part being, *body, soul, and spirit.* The mind is the soul of who you are. This is where your will, feelings, and emotions live. It is your human existence that thrusts you into wholeness. Although your mind operates in concert with your body and spirit, it is ultimately in control of the direction in which you will go, what you will do, and the things that you will have. This is why you need a strong handle on your thoughts, so your decisions will not be based on wrong attitudes, or a thought process that is frequently rehearsing tragedies and hurtful events. Nothing good can ever come from that pattern of thinking.

Each Tuesday evening, I teach these principles and Universal Laws as an after hour's course, and we started out discussing mind renewal. This is the first step in recreating your world for your wealth to be a regular participant in your life. You must change the way in which you think concerning prosperity. YOU MUST LEARN TO CONTROL YOUR OWN MIND! If you don't, someone else will gladly do it for you.

There is a line from a song that was sung back in the 90's by a group called, En Vogue, they sang, "Free Your Mind and the Rest Will Follow." They assert that your mind will lead the way once it is freed. It is imperative to employ your mind to work for you, and then other things will fall in place.

Your mind is designed to expand to the capacity that you are willing to use it.

Many do not take time to nurture their minds or fill it with desires of impossibilities. Trust me! It will be able to handle whatever load you give it by design. With the right thoughts inserted, accomplishing this feat will guarantee your eventual success.

Some time ago, I met a woman who was financially successful in business, and we begin to speak often. She had great insight on financial matters and marketing. After each conversation, I sat with my eyes closed for a few minutes to digest all of the information that she shared with me about achieving impossible objectives. I could literally feel my mind expanding rapidly. During one discussion, I had to ask her to slow down, so I could capture every word that she spoke. Each conversation took me to a new level of which I knew nothing, but it was all that I could think about throughout the day. The knowledge that I obtained is now a part of my thought process forever, and my life is better because I decided to open my mind to prosperity.

Maya Angelou, an American poet and civil rights activist stated, "Do the best you can until you know better. Then, when you know better, do better." That is an invitation to change your direction for the better not to become upset about transforming the way in which you think. Mind renewal is a daily task that is worth the effort and the fight.

The Law of Mind

We have heard the cliché that "the sky is the limit;" know this, "the sky is NOT your limit." You have NO limits! Your only limit may be YOU! If you think that you can't do anything then you can't; if you think that you CAN do anything, then YES! YOU can; contrary to any other belief, your belief is the ONLY one that matters for YOUR goals! An ancient writing tells us, anything that we allow to consume our thoughts will eventually reveal itself in the natural. So, make it a point to reject anything that allows your mind to rehearse limitations and boundaries. Break your limits NOW!

I love the movies "Lucy" and "Limitless." They each display the great possibilities of the Law of Mind but through a foreign substance. Your mind is indeed LIMITLESS without a foreign substance! Although these movies may have been a fictitious depiction of events but they relish the idea to invoke the highest capacity of your mind consciousness to achieve insurmountable heights. YOU must get to

You must acknowledge that you have lived your entire life with negative influences all around you which has governed your experiences with prosperity. However, you can begin today by sweeping those pessimistic powers away through exercising the strength of your mind.

the mental place where you believe that nothing can stand in your way.

For starters, you should first take negative thoughts captive and embark upon a purification of your mind by dumping "old wives tales," pessimistic thoughts, self-guilt, feeling unworthy, harmful family pass downs and anything that symbolizes defeat, destruction, and disorder. I like to call it "mind cleansing" or a reiteration of a positive self-image. You must acknowledge that you have lived your entire life with negative influences all around you which has governed your experiences with prosperity. However, you can begin today by sweeping those pessimistic powers away through exercising the strength of your mind. You can have or be anything that your mind can believe if you begin to upgrade to another level of consciousness. Opposing all others, YOU can have the wealth that you desire!

People are lost in the fog of their own thoughts which keeps their energy and vibration levels low. Therefore, they are not able to attract prosperity when they are on a lower plain. Conversely, on the same level of low energy or vibratory functions are other ills and unfortunate situations which are lurking around to pounce upon you. In order to attract wealth to you, your mind's focus must frequently register positive thoughts so the Law of Attraction can draw nothing but positive things to you.

Open your mind to prosperity NOW! Once you decide what you actually want, then everything around you will start to shift to make what you decided a reality.

But, you need to decide exactly what it is that you want. I have interviewed, instructed, and counseled so many who do not know what they really want. I know it sounds simple enough, but when I ask that question they usually look at me with the "deer stare" or hunch their shoulders while looking blankly through the air. They didn't have a clue of clarity about their future aspirations, dreams, hopes, desires, or what they want or even who they are.

Indecisiveness will delay the good in life from finding you.

Consequently, you will not receive the better life that so many others enjoy. Your outcomes will reflect your indecisive behavior and deliver a never ending cycle of lack. If you can't decide on anything, how can you expect anything to decide to come to you?

Have a "think tank" or a "brainstorm" with yourself. Decide who you desire to become, what does that person look like, and what does that redefined person want out of life. It's often easy to help others decide what their plans should be, but sometimes, it is difficult when the "shoe is on the other foot." Decision and definition are necessary for wealth streams to flow.

If you want to prosper in every area of your life, there are other immediate actions that should be taken. One of those actions is to turn off the television. This entertainment is an insult to the use of your creative mind. By continually seeing commercials, speak to your subconscious mind and put you in the mindset to buy, buy, buy, and spend, spend, spend, which is not what you need to do. Myron Golden, a 21st- Century self-made millionaire and motivational speaker asserts in his book, "From the Trash Man to the Cash Man" that, *"Rich people educate themselves and poor people entertain themselves."* Anyone who has a rich friend can verify that rich people empower themselves through various forms of information that will expand their mind and to stay on the cutting edge of the next level. It is unfortunate that entertainment is a regular pastime for those who are lacking wealth. Entertainment is fine in moderation, but it should not be at the expense of maximizing your highest potential.

Before I became television disciplined an interesting thing happened to me while watching "The Price is Right."A Reese's cup commercial continued to air several times during the hour broadcast. Although I wasn't looking at it directly, I recognized the music each time it aired. A few hours went by, and

I could still hear the music in my head and could taste the soft chocolaty decadence of that Reese's cup. I couldn't take it anymore. I called my husband and asked him to bring me a couple of Reese's cups when he comes home. When he arrived, he had a 6-pack of Reese's cups, and I tore into them as soon as he pulled them out of the bag.

The excitement and ecstatic thrill didn't last too long after that, and then I began to feel violated by the television commercial which I allowed to molest my mind. Not only did it put me in the consumer mode to spend money, but it also desecrated my entire weight loss regiment, because I made the choice to yield to what my eye gate and taste buds desired. The commercial worked on my subconscious and just like that, I became a consumer. How wonderful it would have been if I were actually practicing positive mind exercises that day – the materializing of the Reese's cup could very well have been a Rolls Royce!

Your thoughts are extremely important in obtaining wealth. I often hear people say, "No one cares about what I think." Awkwardly enough, your subconscious mind cares very much what you think and also does exactly what you tell it to do through your words, thoughts, and consistent actions manifesting all that you have expected.

Even though you may feel satisfied with some of your results only because you have been doing the same thing for a long time, know that you are giving away your rights to receive more of what belongs to you simply because you do not want to adjust your mindset. I understand that it requires some discipline but it is possible.

Please realize that if this was easy as 1, 2, 3, then everybody would be onboard but only a few out of many will decide to roll up their sleeves and take a stand to modify their way of life. It will require detoxifying and a reprogramming of the thoughts that you regularly entertain.

Your conscious mind believes only what appears to be definite but your subconscious mind believes anything you impress upon it.

You see, your conscious mind believes only what appears to be definite but your subconscious mind believes anything you impress upon it. It neither has a sense of humor nor does it know when you are joking. It does not know anything other than what you give it with which to work. It can't tell the difference between reality or imaginary projections. We treat our subconscious mind like an unemployed worker, because we pay it little attention. But once you learn to activate the power of this secret weapon regularly, you will be able to manifest things by just passively thinking about them. If you can stimulate your subconscious mind enough to

> *We treat our subconscious mind like an unemployed worker, because we pay it little attention. But once you learn to activate the power of this secret weapon regularly, you will be able to manifest things.*

take hold to your mental thoughts or pictures YOU can experience the wealth of kings.

I remember a statement that computer technician's use to use, "garbage in – garbage out." If most of your thoughts are of lack, poverty, and economic hard times talk your subconscious will ensure that you stay in that posture until you inundate it with something else to process. Neville Goddard, a cosmic philosopher and author, says, "The subconscious transcends reason and is independent of induction." Therefore, you will receive the outcome based on anything YOU feed your subconscious mind no matter how irrational the requests may be. Don't worry; your subconscious mind is the only place where there is never any competition. YOU are the captain and the passenger, so let's get this ship moving!

You may ask how you can impress your subconscious mind to manifest the prosperity that you desire. There are a few things that you can do to train your subconscious mind and hasten your good to come.

-<u>Stay free from negativity</u>
Negative thoughts from the past or present

-<u>Read uplifting material</u>
Disregard news or bad reports/gossip

-<u>Listen to motivational lectures & meditate to music</u>
Play motivational audio while asleep

I have found that these items are very instrumental in keeping the subconscious mind focused on what is pure, perfect and of a good account while working in the direction that will bring all the good that you desire to receive. After sharing these concepts with a woman concerning the purification of mind, she quickly took hold of this exercise and immediately began to apply the steps to her life. When we spoke again, she shared that after activating "mind cleansing" practices, she received an unexpected check of $6,500 within the week! She said she felt much

The subconscious mind is not restricted to any time or space that would prevent your highest good from appearing.

lighter and cleaner as she removed the clutter from her thoughts and vowed to practice purification activities from that moment on.

Her favorite cleansing affirmation used was:

I direct my mind to think of abundance;
my energy empowers my thinking of
sufficiency; my life improves daily; I
release all negative attributes from my
thoughts; I can no longer accept defeat or
limitations; lavish prosperity comes
quickly in all that concerns me NOW.

The subconscious mind is not restricted to any time or space that would prevent your highest good from appearing. In that realm, NOW always takes precedence. After today, condition your subconscious to understand that NOW is always your time to receive!

Whatever you can get your subconscious to believe it will manifest that belief to be a tangible reality. It is your responsibility to give it the BEST directions you can possibly create. Remember, this can work for anyone, because it is a law and YES, it can work for YOU!

There is always an escape plan made no matter how difficult the situation may be or how it might look on the surface. Ancient Greek writings tell us that there is always a way of escape but you should ask for divine wisdom to show you the way.

Receiving divine wisdom is perfect insightful instructions from within that know more than you know and works collectively with your subconscious mind, guiding you towards a favorable outcome. Sometimes we call it a "hunch" or a "gut feeling." Often these "hunches" activate after we have asked for specific guidance but you must pay attention to everything that you see, hear, feel, or sense as they are usually clues to your final answer. If you sense to go somewhere, then go. If someone comes to your mind contact them. If you are told to do something, then do it. Divine wisdom will show you whatever you need to know in order to lead you to your wealth streams.

I often receive preventive commands from divine wisdom but occasionally usurp the final decision depending on the level of importance. In preparing to teach a workshop the night before, I sensed the need to print out my outline in order to take a hardcopy as a backup copy to my iPad. But this time, I brushed it off and consciously thought, "There is no need to take a hardcopy because I have the outline on my iPad." During the workshop the next day, I accidently leaned on my iPad and mistakenly erased the entire outline! I couldn't believe it! All of my information was gone! Having a hardcopy would have served me well, but I didn't listen to the preventive command from within. When you ask for intuitive assistance, don't ignore the instinctive signs that you receive. It may not always make sense to you, but, if you already knew what to do, why ask for help?

On another occasion, I had tried to reach a person for six to eight months but could never reach the right person. I called and left message after message but to no avail. When I awoke one morning, I sensed the hunch to call the person again. When I did, well, wouldn't you know it, after eight months of trying, the right person answered the telephone, and we were finally able to conduct the necessary business at hand which led to a wealth stream. Do you think that it was by coincidence? No, I think not.

You have to learn to listen to the still small voice within to avoid missing out on important cues. There IS an answer to all of your problems, and the Universe is obligated to respond to your voice at all times.

You can start changing NOW! YOU do not have to wait until the beginning of another week, month or a new year to initiate change. NOW is your time!

There is some necessary information that needs to be addressed at the end of this chapter. These exercises are designed to help YOU realize your highest potential and to activate your wealth streams. When used appropriately, you can experience great unmentionable abundance!

Please know that YOU should use these practices to control YOUR OWN MIND not the mind of anyone else! It is spiritually illegal to utilize mind control tactics on others without experiencing any backlash! Save yourself the trouble and focus on YOU!

THE POWER OF YOUR WORDS

(Speaking Prosperously)

Words have power
to change things in your life
exponentially.

The Law of Command

They activate things in the Universe on your behalf according to the words that you speak. It has been suggested that your spoken word of command can bring successful results approximately 85% quicker when used in conjunction with your thoughts.

Whenever you start to talk, the atmosphere begins to shift in conjunction with what you have been declaring in order to bring those things to you. Even if you do not see the immediate results, know that the action has begun and the results are soon to appear as you nurture that which you have spoken. Your words will not return to you void-it will accomplish whatever task it has been sent out to do because YOU said it!

One man shared how he was struggling to pay a bill. He managed to gather three-fourths of the money he needed to pay the bill but it was due that day. He knew the balance due was higher than what he had, which was not sufficient to meet the due date. He remembered a teaching on the

"Power of Your Words" and he selected an affirmation that he could use to level the playing field. Throughout the day, he began to affirm: "All of my financial needs are met because my maximum good is closest to me, and it is sufficient." He knew that something would be done to help him because of the peace he started to feel, but he didn't know how it would be done. Please realize that "the how" is not your responsibility, but believing that everything will work in your favor is.

Once he arrived to pay something on his bill, he asked the representative at the desk could she tell him how much he owed for the month. She looked at his account and told him the balance due. Surprisingly, it was $200 less than he expected to pay. He asked her was she sure that was the correct balance? She smiled and confirmed the balance a second time. He couldn't understand how the balance was so low and wanted to know what happened to the original balance, but she couldn't explain it. He was amazed, overjoyed, and excited all at the same time because he had more than enough to pay the bill and had money to spare. His words proved powerful as he released worry, fear, and doubt from his mind knowing that this situation would somehow work in his best interest – and it did!

A woman who learned the power of the spoken word received an unexpected bank deposit within 24 hours of affirming: "All that belongs to me by divine right will show up at the right time for my use!" She was excited about how quickly this manifestation turned in her favor.

One of my students stated that one of her friends whom she invited to sit in on a session shared that he received an unexpected financial demonstration after practicing affirmations in just one meeting. These are exciting results and can happen for you, too, once you open up your mind to prosperous thinking!

When I started actively using affirmations and practicing prosperous thinking a few years back, I received so many compliments of how youthful I looked and that I was glowing so much that I was asked by a few people if I was pregnant. I thought, "What a laugh!" I was not physically pregnant, but I was spiritually pregnant with possibility, purpose, and the power to change all avenues of my life anyway I chose. I was operating in principles that were doorways to everything that my heart ever desired through the power of my words.

A man stated that he needed $500 to close a deal and he asked if I would speak affirming words to bring it to him. I began to affirm, "I call $500 from the North, South, East and West; I call in unexpected checks, bonuses, overpaid premiums, forgotten and misplaced money, TODAY!" Then I said, "That ought to do it!" He agreed and went home. Later that evening he called to let me know that when he arrived home, there was a $500 check in his mailbox and he was able to close the deal.

These positive words spoken into the atmosphere are often times effective immediately. Whether it is immediate or over a space of time, I dare you to put it to work for you today to experience a windfall of all that you desire. Open your mind to prosperity and effectively apply affirmations to call in the good that belongs to you by divine right.

The Wrong Words

A few years ago I read somewhere that women speak about 8,000 to 10,000 words per day and men about 4,000 words per day . . . what a significant difference! One of the first things you can do to help yourself ignite the good you seek is to cut back on frivolous conversations that are non-purposeful. In most cases you will need to cut off negative discussions with some people to whom you are very close. Don't get caught up in poisonous chatter or judging others unjustly, practice keeping your words as clean as possible to improve your prosperity pipeline and your wealth streams are sure to come.

Do you remember the childhood jingle: "Sticks and stones may break my bones but words can never hurt me?" As I matured in life I discovered that words were just as dangerous, if not more dangerous, as the sticks and stones that the kids sang about.

Negative casual dialogues can kill your wealth streams.

I heard someone say some time ago, that words are like a tube of toothpaste, once the paste is out the tube you can't get it back inside. Therefore, it is imperative that you watch the words that you speak if you do not want to eat them later . . . as they can be bitter.

Those who speak critically about things will see that their words will cause a decrease in the good that they would receive or even stop it from materializing at all. Negative casual dialogues can kill your wealth streams. There is a proverb that says, "Your words will convict you or absolve you." You are ultimately responsible for all that you say because it will show up in your life somewhere. Make sure that they are words with which you can live and you won't mind them returning to you to be rehearsed in your life.

You must minimize unproductive casual talk with friends and family. This is where you give life to negative responses that happens to you. Using negative phrases like, "I can't afford it," "That costs too much," "I'm broke," "I never have enough," "Poor Me," or "Life always deals me a bad hand," will ensure that you have just what you have declared. Instead, use replacement phrases like, "I can afford anything I desire to have,"

By constantly participating in economic hard time discussions, gossip, complaining about others, nothing is ever going right stories and foolish banter speaks volumes to your subconscious mind. It will deliver exactly what you have given it to review.

"What an interesting price; I'll consider purchasing this at a later time," "My funds are temporarily obligated to my other desires," "I am a good steward of my money," or "I am so prosperous," "I enjoy life and make it what I want."

By constantly participating in economic hard time discussions, gossip, complaining about others, nothing is ever going right stories and foolish banter speaks volumes to your subconscious mind. It will deliver exactly what you have given it to review. Another ancient writing says, "You will be trapped by the words that come out of your mouth." When you speak ill of others it will return to you; no words are wasted, even if no one else can hear you saying them! You must ask yourself, "Will this 'freedom of speech' cause me to miss out on my prosperity.

You will have to make the decision to restrict those conversations from your word diet. If you are struggling with this, know that sooner or later you will have to make a decision about this – one way or the other. Because eventually, you will be faced with a choice to limit or ban those who bring negative talk to you. It is going to be up to you ONLY, and sometimes it will be a difficult choice to make, especially if it is your family or close friend.

In order for me to get a handle on this in my life, I literally had to stop giving my time to those who had nothing productive to say and going to particular places where I knew there would be impoverished discussions, negative government news, or senseless conversations. I would only show up, if I absolutely had to be present. Phone calls were limited and many times I did not answer calls.

I stayed away from those who never had anything constructive to say about anything or anybody; these folks were seldom happy anyway. Another thing I did was use my email more to bypass these extra futility situations. It was discovered that most people do not want to write about such folly - they would much rather talk with you about it instead of leaving a paper trail. If you want to experience real prosperity in your life, you need to change the company that you keep and check your words on a regular basis.

Listen to me; if you want to prosper in life, you got to stay away from the influence of negative people. If not, expect the same thing that they have . . . negative influence! This type of connection will cause the Law of Association to take effect. That law suggests that if you associate with five people, who are non-productive, negative, going nowhere in life, always criticizing others, complainers, etc; then by association, you will be the sum total of those five people, which will make you the sixth person in exactly the same "space" as the other five negative and/or impoverished people. Of course, because it is a law, it works the same way with those who are productive, going somewhere in life, positive, speaking well and blessing others, etc. This Law of Association, on the other hand, will cause you to be the sum total of those five positive and/or wealthy people, which will make you the sixth person in exactly the same "space". With which group will YOU choose to associate? Refuse to talk about how difficult some things seem to be. Stop repeating past hurts and experiences that remind you of the worst of times.

When people remember hurtful things from my past and want to intentionally rehearse them with me, they will always start by saying: "Hey, I remember when . . ." It is at that time that I calmly respond: "Yes, I remember too, but I have come a long way since then, so let me bring you up-to-date with the great things that I'm doing NOW!" (Remember "NOW" is always your time.) This response usually shocks them, and I continue reciting all of the positive things that I am currently enjoying which usually diminishes the conversation, unless they, too, have grown since that time.

You are in charge of the atmosphere and vibrations that you want to experience around you. Your words can cultivate that atmosphere.

There was a man who was behind on his mortgage for over nine months. The company would not give him a loan modification and threatened to sell his home if he did not come up with an ungodly amount of money. He received foreclosure letters, but he never spoke any negative words about losing his home, including to his wife. He knew the effect of positive and negative words and declared that he would not lose his home but would receive the money that he so desperately needed in time to prevent the sale of his property.

As the sale date approached, he maintained his declaration and declared the entire day: "All the money I need comes to me at the right time. I cannot lose what is mine by divine right." Miraculously, he was able to secure the exact amount that he needed in order to stop the sale, catch up his mortgage and to remove his home from foreclosure. Because he wanted to be truthful, he finally shared the entire episode with his wife who was overjoyed that it worked out for them!

Your words are important to all situations that concern you. Remember to speak words that affirm what you want to have, become or see yourself doing and watch the flourishing outcome.

As a singer, I have banned singing particular songs because of the repetitive lyrics that often rehearse events of depressing and unsavory experiences. I discovered that the feeling of the song became a part of the emotions that the subconscious mind would take hold; thus giving me the trouble about which I so passionately sang.

Therefore, when I decided to watch my spoken words, I, too, analyzed the songs that I enjoyed repetitively listening to and singing. I realized that songs were also spoken words but strategically put to beautiful music which generated a specific mood or feeling. Many of the songs advocated depression, sickness, violence, poverty, lack and a whole lot of trouble. When I refused to sing them anymore, I noticed a huge emotional uplifting. I felt as though a weight had been lifted from my shoulders, and YES, everything concerning me began to prosper!

Make that decision today to stop living your troubles through songs and take control of your day first thing in the morning by reciting affirmations that will propel your subconscious into overdrive. Think consciously and purposefully about what you say before you say it. Don't take your words for granted or feel that they have little to do with your success. When you find others who speak cavalierly, don't get sucked into their rhetoric! Give much thought to the right words to use.

If you need reminders write out your good, prosperous thoughts on index cards and carry them around with you. Post them on your bathroom mirrors, refrigerator, and anywhere you spend a lot of time to saturate your mind with those things that are of substance. Take every opportunity to provoke mind renewal. Every word matters!

Writing Your Thoughts Down

A practice that I use to activate wealth streams is writing out what I desire, and a plan of what I expect to happen. Some call it "scripting, journaling or lettering." This process has about a 90% rate of return of receiving the desires that you request in conjunction with speaking affirmations. It serves YOU well to list deliberate thoughts on paper to assist with your desires coming to fruition.

At the beginning of each year, I have preferred this method versus quoting unreasonable New Year's resolutions that are often broken by March of the same year. Use this technique to write out your impossible ideas and dreams without sharing them with everyone. Sometimes your mind will change about the things you write down and that's okay. You can make revisions. As your thoughts mature, you are free to rearrange your list of priorities, but at least you have an outline with which to redevelop as often as you would like. Are you applying these principles yet? If not, what are you waiting for, get started!

One woman stated that she was grateful to have learned the method of writing her thought-out desires on paper because it kept her focused on her thoughts. It also served as a reminder of what she requested and how quickly it appeared after writing it down. Writing your thoughts and vision down forces you to consciously pinpoint exactly what it is that you really want; then your world will begin to reshape based on your definitive plans. Ensure that you are writing down those plans that are truly your heart's desire and that it is truly what you want, not only for what you think you can have. Otherwise, your results will yield an undesired response. I like the way that writing calls you to action. It causes you to make a DECISION about your truth without musing over how it will be done! Even as I write this book my life is changing for the better.

Let's discuss this example. You decide that you want to move up in your organization. Firstly, please ensure that you are doing what your current position requires of you to do. Next, write down the type of promotion that you want; the location, the pay that you desire and the improvements that you would like to make without criticizing the person(s) who may be in that position currently. (Why didn't I practice this technique years ago)? Be prepared to implement your written plan when the time for promotion becomes available or if you are asked for ideas that will enhance the overall composition of the organization. That is the time that you can release the ideas that you have had in order to expand your company's net worth. Treat it like your life depended on it and you will receive what you put in it. If you want a better life, list the things that would make your life better. If it is more money, list exactly how much money you desire to have. Simply saying, "I want to be a millionaire by Tuesday" is not the way to approach this endeavor. Perhaps saying, "I will be a millionaire by Tuesday, on December 31st, 20___ and here are the ways in which I will attain this goal." Then, make a list of the realistic ideas that flashes through your mind and write them down. Your subconscious mind will work in concert with you to bring all of your definite ideas to completion. You

Your greater good wants to connect with you as much as you want to connect with it.

will discover that your greater good wants to connect with you as much as you want to connect with it. To deny or ignore that you have these cravings for a better life can turn into unpleasantries that will render negative responses because of your inability to release these flourishing thoughts from deep within yourself. Writing it down can cleanse your mind of clutter and disorganization.

If you have things that you desire to see removed from your life or matters that you hope would dissolve or go away, then this process is equally as helpful as it is for those things that you do want. Make a list of the undesired issues and declare over it, "You are dismissed! Be gone!" This will work with bad business deals, stressful conditions, disagreements, worn out relationships or any unpleasant hard place that you may experience. Write it down and watch it dissolve!

I gave this exercise to my students. I asked them to write out a daily list of items that they wished to have realized or dissolved that day. They were advised to practice this procedure soon after they awoke and before their day started. This gave direction to their mind which worked in conjunction with their words and deepest feelings. Then, I asked them to write down a list of as many impossible things as they could that they expected to have realized at some point in their lifetime. This list was comprised of all of the things that they wanted to see happen either in a short time frame or sometime in the distant future and the results were phenomenal! I enjoyed the conversations, emails and phone calls that I'd received as a result of this practice. In addition, they in turn, enjoyed the fruits of their writing it down!

When you practice this exercise, please, do not worry about "how" it will happen or even when; but simply look for your subconscious mind to lead you in the right direction to make it work together for your good. You will begin to scratch items off of your list as your daily task will somehow be accomplished with ease. Write your thoughts and vision down and make your planned results clear, so if anyone is asked to read it, then they would understand how you accomplished your objective. More so, you will be able to understand your ideas and accomplish every task you set out to do.

If you find yourself in a place where you are not able to speak your affirmations out loud, the writing aspect is often a grand replacement of activities. Whatever spoken affirmations you have been reciting, you may also write them down in succession to keep your thoughts centered and responsive. Ensure to keep notepads, tablets, journals, or a whole lot of paper handy to express your desires through this form of constantly reminding yourself of the good you expect.

There is one more thing that I have discovered that works handsomely for me, and that is recording my voice. I record my voice as I recite affirmations that are relevant to whatever I need to quickly manifest for me. Once I record the affirmations that I desire, I transform them into an MP3 file and play them on repeat from the time I lay down for sleep until the time I awake in the morning. I keep the volume turned down at the lowest level to avoid disturbing my husband's rest. Even though it is not blaringly loud, my subconscious can still hear the recording of affirmations and work through the night without once disturbing my slumber because it never sleeps. When I awake I feel like running through the city while doing somersaults because I feel that good! The practice of the non-stop recording of what I have affirmed played all night in the ethers and directed my mind to bring to me exactly what I've affirmed. Plus, it sweetens my dreams each night!

You can record affirmations to bring your good to you and remove the bad from you. You can record school notes to help you prepare for your upcoming tests; Scripture to fulfill any spiritual desires; instructions to keep your life in divine order; or anything that you want your subconscious to actively work on for you during the four to eight hours that you are sleeping. This gives your subconscious that much of a head start before your conscious mind awakens to rationalize anything. This is down time well utilized and can only add to your success and prosperity of life.

At the end of this book you will find additional affirmations that you can use for various situations. You can use them separately or in conjunction with any of the other affirmations to accommodate any of your desires.

Make this daily 45 second affirmation over your lists for 15 minutes:

This day was created just for me to excel as I am unlimited. Divine wisdom shows me all that I should know in every situation. Prosperity follows me in every phase of my life, as I am favored and empowered to change my world. My life is in divine order and I am full of joy and peace. All that belongs to me by divine right comes to me at the right time, and it does not impede the good of anyone else. My financial income increases. As money is used it immediately circulates back to me in perfect ways. I expect my desires to return to me in an equal or a better distribution than I've asked. I am victorious and loved. I am a magnet for all good things.

The Power of Your Imagination

(Visualizing Your Prosperity)

Every end result

starts off as an idea.

When you see landscapes, clothes, food, buildings, inventions and even YOU, each finished product started off as a thought. All things created were first conceived in the mind of someone who ultimately gave life to the picture that they saw in their mind's eye. It's called the

IMAGINATION. I can tell if I will be successful in any situation based on how clearly I can see the picture in my mind. If I can't get a clear visual, the outcome resembles the same, little to no success, but when I get a clear visual of events, that picture yields an astounding outcome.

Children have little challenge imagining things. They talk to invisible people, do invisible things with them and go to invisible places. It happens all in their minds.

When I was a kid, I used to imagine that my cat could talk and understand what I was saying. We spent several hours communicating as she purred softly around my ankles. I loved the time alone even though I had six older siblings and a neighborhood full of children with whom to play "hide and seek." However, I found great peace and creativity during this time of reflection. I used this same imagination when I had to write stories in my classes. One of my teachers marveled at my creative imagination because it was always so vivid and colorful; no one could tell a story more captivating than I could.

At that time, I didn't know the power that I possessed early in life that would bring anything to me through my imagination. But before I could grasp that concept, I became poisoned by teachings of society; like, if you talk to yourself and answer yourself; you are fit for a straight jacket. Or if you spend too much time with your head in the clouds you will get nothing accomplished by dreaming because it will never come true. Although I am a visual learner, unfortunately, I let those comments dampen my ideas of seeing the impossible things that I desired, but thankful to God it didn't completely dissolve my ability to dream. After some years of renewing my mind, and disregarding negative comments, I was able to imagine the impossible once again and now it is really easy for me to visualize the good that I want. It is said, "If you have no vision you will eventually fade into a life of mundane rituals and practices like some others". . . and that is what can happen to YOU if you allow others to talk

By using the imagination process, you can supply your subconscious mind with all of the good things that you would like to see manifested in the natural.

you out of your dreams, ideas and wealth streams.

By using the imagination process, which is the technique of visualization (we will use this word interchangeably), you can supply your subconscious mind with all of the good things that you would like to see manifested in the natural. This is also an opportunity to keep your thoughts flooded with your desired good in order to outweigh any negative pictures that you may have rehearsed over the years. The more you develop your visualization of positive images; the more positive demonstrations will come quicker to you.

The secret to this process is to picture yourself already with whatever manifestation that you are asking to receive. Trust me. I am working on my own pictures as I write out this manuscript. If it's a new house that you desire to have, then decide where you want it to be located, the color of the exterior, whether it is brick, aluminum or stucco, and the style it should be. See yourself out in the front yard chasing the dog or walking through the house into the large master bedroom, or a glass shower with ceramic tile, or cooking in your industrial kitchen or eating in the sunroom, or playing air hockey in the game room, or smelling the new leather furniture in the living area, or simply lying out on the deck catching some sun. I hope that I painted a vivid picture for you so you can experience the visual that I saw when I wrote it. Can you see yourself doing any of those things? If not, let's try another example.

If you desire a new car, decide which type of car that you want and know that you can have it no matter what your bank account says or your credit report dictates. Just be free with your visualization without any hindrances. So, let's say you want a SLK 350 charcoal gray Mercedes Sports. You need to see yourself in that car riding on the highway with the top down as the sun radiates on your skin and your choice of music is playing on your stereo. Hear the horns honking at you as you pass other vehicles. Feel how tight the steering wheel is as you turn it (because it's new), get a whiff of that new car leather smell; feel how comfortable the cushioned leather seats are, but make sure you stay under the speed limit because you've spotted a blue and white police car traveling two cars behind you. Can you see yourself in the car, experiencing the above outcome? Until you can see yourself with it, then it will be very difficult for YOU to materialize it. Put your imagination to work for you – it's one of the only FREE things left!

One of my favorite childhood stories was "Alice in Wonderland." It was a dark fairytale, yet a fascinating story nonetheless. In the modern day "Alice" I love the phrase, "I think about six impossible things every day before breakfast," and I remember reading where someone else ended it by saying, ". . . and I accomplish five of them."

Can you imagine practicing the technique of visualization or will you let doubt cheat you out of this profound experience? How many times have you just received what you were told and believed that you couldn't have what you desired because someone else, **who has nothing,** said it was IMPOSSIBLE? If that's the truth for you, then know that you have the power to change your current situation through visualization NOW!

Another exercise I use to speed up the good in my life is a vision board, vision books, or as other visualization gurus call it "A Wheel of Fortune." I have all three. I have affirmations on index cards and pictures taped to my bathroom mirror to remind me of the good that I desire. I keep it before my physical eyes and peripheral vision as often as possible to constantly saturate my subconscious mind with an abundance of "good stuff."

This is how this process worked for me. I made a vision board identifying six areas of my life in which I desired good to flow. I wanted to get rid of two display cases that I owned from a business, and I was ready to sell them to reduce the size of my storage unit. They had been listed online for three years and no one offered to buy them. I was frustrated and about to give them away when I decided to practice my own methods of visualization. I cut out a picture of the display cases and glued it to my vision board. I then sat quietly, initially for about twenty minutes imagining the entire exchange from beginning to end. Then, I kept it on the forefront of my mind throughout the day as I continued to affirm, "I call the right buyer in for these display cases for the right price so they may serve you as well as they have served me, and both parties are happy about the exchange." As I affirmed what I wanted I simply began to visualize what I expected to happen. I imagined a truck pulling up to my storage unit and taking both displays away. Then I saw myself sweeping out the storage unit while happily humming a tune; that was the expected end result. Within 48 hours of posting the photos on my vision board and visualizing this much desired transaction, someone called and offered to buy both displays AFTER 3 YEARS of trying to rid myself of them!

We met the buyers and just like I visualized, they pulled their truck up to the unit door and carefully loaded the displays on it. They paid for the items and both parties were happy about the exchange. The only thing that was left for me to do was to sweep out the storage unit – and I did that a few days later while happily humming a tune. Taking time to visualize the positive outcome that you long for can hasten your desired results.

There is a song by the Temptations called, "Just My Imagination." Eddie Kendricks sang this entire song about a woman whom he'd often watched.

Throughout the song, he explained what their lives would be like. They would have a cozy home in the country and would be married with children. He painted such a brilliant picture concerning his thoughts, hopes, and dreams so real that WE thought they were actually somehow true. But he finally shares the reality that the woman didn't even know he existed. The point is that he so skillfully described in great detail what he desired to happen. He described the picture so well that we could actually visualize their future together; how much he loved her and almost what the kids would look like. Can you describe all of the good that you desire in such detail as this song depicted? Can you adequately paint a picture so life-like that it will cause your subconscious mind to bring it to fruition? If not, then YOU have much work to do!

Remember, you have to SEE it before you SEE it.

I will share one of my visual experiences of making the right car purchase after having two visions (I will talk more about visions and dreams in another book very soon).

In August 2012, my car was flooded out in a storm that no one knew was coming. When my husband woke me early that morning, it was still raining and the water was up to the hood of my car. I looked at it and said, "Only God can do anything about that," and I went back to bed. When I woke again my husband wanted to know my plans for a new vehicle, I told him that I was not interested in a new vehicle as my flooded car was paid off for several years, and I did NOT want any new payments. It is to this end that one of my friends let me borrow her car just so I could get around. I was just as happy about that with no thought of a new vehicle. A few days later, it rained again and flooded my car a second time in the same fashion. The one thing I could say was, if there was any doubt that this car was totaled, the second rain storm proved that I would never crank it up again.

After a couple of days went by, I met a man who haphazardly began to talk about cars and how his son worked at a local dealership. He didn't know about my car incident, but he told me if I ever needed a car to go see his son. I was still somewhat unconcerned about purchasing a new vehicle, but I took the business card and put it in my purse anyway. About a week later, something interesting happened to me. As I slept, I had a vision of being at a car lot, standing in front of a big picture window with my hands on my hips. I woke up in the morning, shook off what I'd seen and went about my day. The next night, I had the same exact vision of standing in front of this big picture window with my hands on my hips. When I woke the next morning, I was rather concerned and knew I had to do something.

When you receive dreams, visions, given a hunch to go somewhere, or do something, no matter how insignificant it might seem; never ignore it! You will find that these sensations are doorways to the good for which you need to open for you.

I didn't want to wait for the third vision the next night; therefore, I asked for divine wisdom to show me the location of the car dealer that I saw in the vision. I was then reminded to get the card out of my purse that I'd put there a week earlier and immediately drove to that lot.

When I drove on the lot, I called the representative by phone whose name was on the card, but he said he was off that day and advised me to look around and see if there's something that I would like to purchase and to come back the next day. It's interesting that he used the word, "purchase." It was almost like he knew I would buy a car before I knew I would. So I drove around the lot for a few minutes and looked at Aston Martins, Mercedes and other high powered cars that I couldn't pronounce and grew even more frustrated with the search as I knew that I would not return the next day. I was literally acting like a spoiled brat! However, after talking with my husband, he strongly encouraged me to find a car that I liked, and he would meet me at the lot the next day to ensure that I did just that. He knew, eventually, I would want to borrow his vehicle and he was not at all interested in that exchange.

Now, the next day I went back to the car lot and my husband met me there as he stated he would. We got in one car to test drive it, and it rode rather nicely. When we returned to the car lot I parked the car and was asked, "What type of car do you want?" (Remember, we must make a decision as to what we really desire.) I responded, "I really don't know!" I looked at every car that I could see and examined all colors but still didn't know what I wanted. So, I got out of the car and stood in the parking lot to ponder what I wanted. After a little conversation I put my hands on my hips and I looked in the big picture window of the dealership that I saw in my vision and there was a car right on the showroom floor! I knew it was the one because it felt so right. I pointed to it and said, "I want that one!"

One of the funniest things about this story is that we had to walk past the car in the showroom window about fifteen times to go in and out of the dealership, and I never once noticed the car sitting there. It did not reveal itself to me until I was standing in the right place – in the exact place that I'd seen in the two visions. I must say, it was the easiest car deal I've ever made in my life, and I drove off the showroom floor with only twelve miles registered on the dash. What an excellent experience! O, and the car payments; well, I don't have enough room in this book to explain how miraculous that situation worked out in my favor!

I remember reading this statement recently, "If you want to stop someone, give them different visions." As you read earlier, I received two visions, but they were identical. No one is able to follow two visions effectively as their mind's eye will be divided. One of the ancient writings says: "If you have two mindsets you cannot expect to receive anything for which you hope." You must be definite about what you really want to receive in order to receive it. Once you have identified the main thing, you should focus on that which you desire to bring it closer to you. Then, you will see it manifest itself. You may ask just how long does it take for a manifestation of good to appear? It is said, "the light of the body is the eye" and until your mind's eye is single and focused on what you desire, that is the time frame. It's all up to YOU!

Don't ever try to rush or force a picture to appear, just let it happen. It should be as natural as blinking your eyes, as it will flow through your thoughts by flashes or a passing picture. If your head or eyes began to hurt, you are trying too hard. Allow pictures to flash into your subconscious mind periodically. Take hold of what your words and inner self creates for you. Visualize what you desire, in as much detail as you can. Know that you may create anything that your mind can conceive or picture. This proves most effect when you are getting prepared to go to sleep at night and upon waking in the morning. Your subconscious mind will begin to work these creations out for you as you slumber. Whatever you want your mind to manifest, start thinking about it right before you go to sleep. You can use the affirmation: "I now accelerate my good by imaging it. This is effortless for me, as I can see myself with all of the good that I desire and it looks great on me and with me."

You may also alter things in your mind that you can see. If you can see yourself losing weight you would need to imagine or see yourself at the desired weight you choose. If you see yourself taking a special vacation to the islands or some other country you should prepare to travel. You may need a passport or some new luggage but start preparing yourself for where you want to go and imagine yourself being there while feeling the

Your imagination is not able to think logically because it doesn't rationalize ideas or thoughts which allow you to create the type of world that you long to have.

experience as if it has already happened for you.

It may sound silly to do but I say, at least try it to prove that it doesn't work. Those who have little positive imagination will tell you, "This is ridiculous" or tell you, "You can't afford this trip." I say to you, "What do you have to lose?" Everyone has an imagination, but many do not imagine the good to which they are entitled because they usually allow the pain and pressures of life to inundate their daily thought process, therefore, rendering them unfavorable outcomes of pain and pressure rather than pleasure and prosperity as a result.

Your imagination is not able to think logically because it doesn't rationalize ideas or thoughts which allow you to create the type of world that you long to have. It is time well used to sit quietly everyday to imagine all the nice things that you would like to have by visualizing impressive pictures to submerge your subconscious mind.

I am a Ms. Pac Man junkie. In the 80's that was my game of choice at any convenient store that had it available. I really enjoyed the speed of the game and scored over 200,000 points occasionally and "looped" several screens. I've always wanted one at my house but knew my parents would never approve of the purchase, plus the arcade game was really expensive in those days.

Several years went by, and I still had a desire to own one but only thought about it off and on in passing. One year, someone asked me what I wanted for my birthday. Without a thought, I shouted excitedly, "I want a Ms. Pac Man machine" and thought nothing else of it. A few weeks went by and a delivery truck pulled up to my house and delivered a Ms. Pac Man machine and not just any machine, this machine was a 1982 Namco Limited arcade style machine with over thirty arcade games programmed in it! Every 80's video game that I used to play was now at my fingertips forever. They included, of course, Ms. Pac Man, Pac-Man, Jr., Donkey Kong 1, 2 (Foundry), and 3, Tetris, Pac-Man Plus, Frogger, Pengo, Super Pac-Man, Galaga, Galaxian, Zaxxon, Mr. Do's Castle, Burger Time and the list goes on. I was in video heaven, and I still play it today. I can stop and start games over and over no matter how many times without having once to put a quarter in the slot!

The craving to have this game was still in my subconscious mind after many years. I knew what I wanted, and I never let it disappear, so it finally materialized. Yes, it did take some time, but I was not focused on it every day; yet, it came to me as a GIFT! Just imagine if I had visualized the machine on a daily basis; it would have come to me much quicker. I think I may need the arcade style Pole Position race car game now to complete my set!

And, of course, this works along the same lines for financial increase. If you desire to have extra money you can cause it to materialize for you. Open up the inner eye of your mind and see yourself with whatever amount of money that you desire to see. Imagine buckets and barrels full, trash bags overflowing with cash. Hear the sound of the teller counting the $100 bills, smell the ink, and feel the texture of each new bill. Then visualize sitting in the bank counting the stacks of money you put inside your briefcase while reviewing your bank statement that is in the black around the six or seven figure range. See yourself being comfortable with the idea of financial abundance. Can you see it? Can you hear it? Can you feel it? Can you smell it? Utilize the examples in this chapter and began to develop the imagination muscles in your mind!

The Power of Your Giving

(Circulating Your Prosperity)

Live to Give!

In a world where everyone has his hand out for this and that many cringe at the idea of giving anything to anyone. Society has created an amalgamation of those who continuously look for handouts or something for free, but soon find out that free is not always free as there will eventually be something redeemed on the backend.

There is no such thing as getting something for nothing. An old proverb asserts, "You cannot get another breath until you have given one away." As giving one breath to receive another breath is mandatory to live, the fraternal twins, giving and receiving, likewise requires a mandatory exchange.

No matter what attitude you take about giving, please know that giving guarantees receiving.

No matter what attitude you take about giving, please know that giving guarantees receiving. The caveat to that is ANYTHING that you give will surely come back to you. Many call this type of circular phenomenon, "karma" or "what goes around comes around." In old ancient writings, it is called "sowing and reaping," scientifically known as, the Law of Reciprocity. Remember, when it's a law, it will work for anyone and toward anything that you give – whether it is good stuff or bad stuff, it will eventually come back around to you.

I consider this as one of my bonus chapters because I was not going to put this topic in this book. However, it solidifies the previous chapters as a sure way to receive multiplied prosperity in your life. It has to work, because it is a law!

Let's look at some of the things that we can give. We can give love or hate, help or hurt, offense or forgiveness and other emotions that we may not realize we are expressing, and yes, we can offer material things as well.

Giving activates something else that is called the Law of Vacuum. When you release things that you don't want or no longer have use for, it opens up a clear path for the good things that you desire. This law fills the empty space that you have created by giving or releasing your good.

Sometimes we can identify what we have given based on the things that we have in our lives, some good things and some not so good things. This should encourage you to give more of whatever it is that you desire to receive. Basically, if you want to receive good will, good emotions or good things, including money, give out the same good as though it were you on the receiving end, but do it wisely.

Giving activates something else that is called the Law of Vacuum. When you release things that you don't want or no longer have use for, it opens up a clear path for the good things that you desire. This law fills the empty space that you have created by giving or releasing your good. Aristotle, an ancient Greek philosopher and scientist is credited for expressing that "nature abhors a vacuum," while others recite that "the

Universe abhors a vacuum." In either sense this empty space must be filled regardless of the correctness of the terminology. It doesn't matter how you believe or whether or not you believe at all, it will not change the operation of this law in your life when put to task. If you want something it would be in your best interest to give more of that which you want to receive.

I love telling this particular story of how the Law of Vacuum operated for me. I decided one day to clean out my closets and drawers. There were so many items that I had not worn in years, that I'd collected over six oversized trash bags and I gave them all away and released them by saying, "You have served your purpose for me and now I release you to serve someone else." Within two weeks of scooting those bags out of my house someone, who was not aware of my closet cleaning festivities, called and said that they wanted to buy me some clothes; I was excited! They told me that they had a magazine that I could pick out whatever clothes I wanted – and believe you me, I did! The Law of Vacuum was at work to replace what was missing in my life. The items I received were newer, prettier and fit so much better and other new clothing items are still coming from various sources all because I started the process of creating a vacuum! Of course, this works for anything that you release because the void must be filled!

Some have asked me when giving money, to who should they give their financial support since there is so many worthy places in which to give. My response to them is that I give where I am receiving spiritual inspiration that changes my life exponentially and also those places where my passions are supported. So I say to you the same, give where you feel a connection to the mission, vision and passion of an entity or person that ignites and inspires your purpose. Never be forced, manipulated, or coerced to give anywhere that you do not feel a correlation – giving should be a cheerful experience and you should have enjoyment as you jubilantly disburse those goods. When good returns to you, I'm sure that you want those goods to come back to you cheerfully and with great enjoyment.

Giving of Yourself

There are some who feel that they have nothing to give. As I travel, often I meet people who express similar sentiments. However, I explain to them that each of us retain gifts that we can offer to others for the betterment of mankind. When you utilize the gifts that you possess it will bring prosperity to you as you will be fulfilled. Russell Conwell suggested in his book, Acres of Diamonds that, "Your wealth is too near to you. You are looking right over it!" Whenever you think that you have to look elsewhere for inspiration, simply look within yourself – many times you have overlooked what is right in your own backyard.

One example of this was experienced by a man who needed some extra cash to do some things without having to use what he already had delegated to go elsewhere. So he thought to himself, "How can I get some extra money, quickly and LEGALLY" and then dismissed it. That night he had a dream that reminded him of what he possessed. The dream was full of musicians, music, and singers with dialogue that gave him clear direction. When he awoke from the dream, he knew how he could quickly make some extra money . . . it was by using his gifts as a musician and as a singer. When he understood the interpretation of the dream, he said, "All musical opportunities that are mine by divine right quickly come to me NOW!" Within a few days, opportunities quickly came rushing into him so much that he had to give some of the opportunities away. He opened himself to divine wisdom and received an answer that he had long overlooked. What he needed was found within himself, his gift to make people happy through his musical talents, which brought him the money that he needed to accomplish some things.

This example could have been listed under any of the above chapters but I chose to put it here to show that we always have something to give . . . our service. In his book, Think and Grow Rich, Napoleon Hill surmises: "If you are dissatisfied with what you are receiving, check the service that you are giving." I add to that by saying, "Your results are decided by your service and your service is guided by your true heart's desire." Whenever you give, you will always receive something in return whether you think of receiving or not. Look within yourself to discover your wealth streams.

Receiving Your Good

Earlier in this chapter, I called giving and receiving fraternal twins. This is to show how different they are; yet, they must work together to complete the cycle. They are contingent upon one another. It's like the "yin and yang," receiving brings balance to giving as it co-exists with giving; yet, has a different operation. Although giving is always discussed as the only altruistic service receiving can also be a means of philanthropic opportunity. Unfortunately, it is casually shunned because of the seemingly selfish kickback for doing "good deeds" for others.

I often hear many say they NEVER give to receive. Somehow, I only believe this about 98% of the time anyway as I find that people generally like to say what they think is popular to the masses. It is considered, "false humility."For, it is impossible to give without receiving regardless of the intended purpose or even if the latter is ignored. It is a law.

Now, make no mistake about the ways of prosperity, it is never designed for anyone to operate in greed. This is not a method to build bigger barns simply to store or hoard riches as this will only bring temporary pleasure. Our wealth is intended to be shared to help others along the way, restore order where there is chaos, and influence the world for a greater purpose.

For many years I had a hard time receiving from others for several reasons. One reason was because I was always suspicious of others motives and wanted to know what they wanted in return. Then I felt that I didn't need anything from anybody. I have since understood what the latter apprehension was called . . . "PRIDE!" I didn't realize that I was stopping my good from getting to me and their good from getting to them simply because I didn't know how to receive. We are often told, "It is better to give than to receive," which is truth. However, it does not mean that you should never be on the receiving end as it would negate the entire idea of giving as SOMEONE must be a receiver! Receiving allows "the receiver" to attain his good desires and it affords "the giver" the opportunity to make room for more of what he desires as the process is set in motion to share the abundance of wealth.

Some years ago, I was preparing to go to France. I had yet to secure my airplane ticket. About a month before my trip, I received a telephone call from a woman who heard that I was traveling abroad and wanted to know if I had purchased my airplane ticket yet. I told her how busy my schedule had been and I didn't have time to look for my ticket. I told her I still had a few weeks before my travel time, so I would get around to it sooner or later. Then she said, "When you find the flights you want, let me know and I will secure the ticket for you!" Although it was a nice and incredible gesture, I almost didn't accept the offer. But I remembered the giving and receiving factor and consented to the purchase! "Wow!" I thought. How wonderful and timely.

Within a day or so, I received another telephone call from another woman who also knew of my trip abroad. She offered to cover my hotel expenses. Of course, this was much easier to receive. I was indeed on the receiving end. My entire trip had been paid! It's to this end that I have periodically checked in on the lives of both of these women and

> *In order to unclog your prosperity channels, you will also need to learn the system of receiving from others to work in conjunction with Universal laws that activate the reciprocity process.*

discovered that neither of them wanted for anything! They each continued to receive windfalls of unexpected good as they were never without the things that they desired.

In order to unclog your prosperity channels, you will also need to learn the system of receiving from others to work in conjunction with Universal laws that activate the reciprocity process. Please understand that this is not a practice of voracity or overindulgence, but it is the circulation of wealth. Someone has to give and someone has to receive.

When the quarterback throws the football it can never be a touchdown unless there is someone available to receive it. As you give, you will receive and the cycle is never broken.

THE POWER OF YOUR GRATITUDE

(Just Thankful)

Do you know of anyone who is critical about everything and everybody?

They complain about persons, places and things? Well, those people are easy to spot. Watch their lives and you will discover that things around them simply do not prosper. They lack the "attitude of gratitude." They tend to look over the everyday common blessings and become critical of not having enough. Not once being thankful for the things in life that they already possess.

There is always something good that can be found in any situation. If you are reading this, please pause to realize just how fortunate you are, barring any current obstacles that you may be facing. Let's see, you are able to read this book, buy it or someone was kind enough to get it for you; you can see, possibly comprehend the material and got all the way to this chapter; oh, and by the way, YOU ARE ALIVE! Those are just a few things for which to be thankful. Being critical of things or people has never generated the wherewithal to sustain prosperity in your life, and it will kill your wealth streams.

When I was a kid I was taught to say, "Thank You" if someone gave me something or did something nice for me. I have learned in every situation to find something for which to be thankful.

Have you ever received an item of clothing that you didn't like, and you tried to find a way to get rid of it? Have you ever received an ugly sweater, unattractive shoes, even food that you didn't like? I've discovered that even if you do not prefer the item that you were given, it is always in order to say, "Thank You" and show appreciation for the thought that was put into giving you that item. "Thank You" goes a long way.

I have found that those who do not express heartfelt appreciation are usually the most miserable creatures on the face of this planet. This simple response carries weight in the process of receiving.

Many times, I have given to others and never received a "Thank You" from them. Not that I gave to be recognized; yet, noticeable enough to draw attention to the lack of appreciation on their part.

One person I gave something to felt that it was my obligation to do what I did for her; she took my kindness for granted and never looked back. However, I did not allow her attitude to stop me from continuing to give to others. Even though that experience was somewhat hurtful, I quickly released the hurt, forgave, and continued to give regardless of the absence of gratitude.

And let me say this, when you give sometimes, people might not always respond the way you think they should. This is why you have to give from your heart.

For my past birthday's, I'd received several gifts and cards from some wonderful people and I made it a practice to bless each card and gift that I received from everyone. I would speak kind words of appreciation and thanks for the person and their household for their endeavor to give. As a result, I often heard how they received equal or better gifts of appreciation from others to replace what that had given me. You can never over appreciate the art of appreciation.

Every morning, I follow a blessing and gratitude exercise before my feet hit the floor. I begin to list ten to fifteen things for which I am thankful. First it sounded mundane, "I bless and thank you God for my life, I bless and am thankful for my health, I bless and am thankful for the activities of all of my limbs and the articulation of speech." Then I start to feel the results of my appreciation. All of a sudden something inside me seems to burst at the seams and I get the "teary eye" because I realize that it could have been another way. Then I jump right into blessing and being thankful for my husband and children, and my extended family. By this time, I am a "weeping willow." Rarely am I able to get to the material things that I possess before crying my eyes out.

You see, these are the things most important in my life. The love that we share, the incredible memorable moments that are picture perfect and priceless, the things that can never be re-lived are at the top of my list daily. If I can pull myself together, I then continue with other important persons, places, and things. Usually this time of reflection lasts about an hour or so before I grace the world with my excitement and enthusiasm!

I have often declared appreciation for things that have yet to happen. I call it my "in advance appreciation." My husband made a statement concerning this type of gratitude. He made the point that at meal time, many people are in the practice of blessing and being thankful for their food before they even taste it. They don't even know if it will be appetizing, too hot, or too cold, or if it needs salt or pepper. Whatever the case may be, they say a prayer to bless it before they even taste it. I thought to myself if you can bless and be grateful for food that has yet to be tasted then it can be done for other things before they are received. I've discovered, it really works!

Although I've always practiced gratitude, I made it a point to get better at it. When I became grateful for things that I had yet to receive as though they were already in my possession, I must say, within a short period of time; they were in my possession. For each morning as I practiced this exercise, I attached my visualization process with it. I see myself with these things, holding them, caring for them, and enjoying them!

In activating your wealth streams this form of appreciation is connected with the art of receiving.

In activating your wealth streams this form of appreciation is connected with the art of receiving. When you are expecting to acquire anything one must ask himself have you been thankful for what you already have received?

I would often tell people that they had to teach their minds to be grateful and bless all of the good that they desire even if they have yet to receive it. Even when I see a lonely penny or any other coin on the ground I stop and pick it up because I am thankful for it; and I bless it!

One day, my husband and I were eating at a diner. When we sat down at the table, I noticed a penny on the floor between our table and another table. So, I casually leaned over, picked it up with thanksgiving and blessed it. I placed it on the corner of our table, just in case someone wanted to use or claim it. After the meal, my husband went to pay the check but quickly rushed back to the table. He asked me did I have .05 cents because the bill was $22.05 and he wanted to pay exact cash. So I opened my wallet to check my change. When I looked inside, I pulled out four pennies and thought, "Wow! I am a penny short. I only have four pennies." But then I remembered the penny that I put on the corner of our table and it was still there. I said, "YES, I have five pennies!" That one penny was exactly what I needed at the right time. What a difference a penny can make! You may call me crazy being thankful for one penny but I have learned the secrets of being thankful. Remember, pennies make dollars and all money is necessary money!

The Power of Your Forgiveness
(A Life of Freedom)

Are you experiencing

blockage in any area of

your life?

Does it seem like you have given and given and conditioned your mind to receive all the good things that belong to you by divine right but it still seems that the magnitude of your good that you know you are entitled to somehow continually escapes your grasp? Well, perhaps this is a chapter that you might want to give more of your attention.

We have been told that our emotional state has a direct correlation to our health and well-being. Scientists have studies that prove that harsh emotions such as anger, resentment, bitterness, and unforgiveness are often the base of various illnesses and maladies.

I remember some years ago speaking with a woman who possessed one of these harsh emotions against someone and soon developed an unhealthy condition in her intestines, which was not a normal condition for someone under the age of thirty. After counseling, she knew that she would need to dispose of the emotion that poisoned her system from the start, if she really wanted her situation to change. When she decided to change her mindset and began to declare positive health and forgiveness affirmations, she was able to release the negative emotion that she harbored. Then her condition cleared and did not resurface. She is now much happier, healthier, and prosperous!

Forgiveness is an act that will not only free you from a life of bondage, but it also frees the mind and the atmosphere between you and those who have offended you. It is necessary to establish that offense can be received or rejected; it is a personal choice. Author and psychologist, J. Martin Kohe says in his book, Your Greatest Power, "The greatest power that a person possesses is the power to choose." When others are operating in offense you have the ability to reject the poison that is being delivered to you. These offenses can be hurtful words spoken to you or over you, accusations against you, or simply an air of an attitude that rubbed you the wrong way. Regardless of the category in which it may fall, receiving offense and mulling over it is toxic and can impede the prosperity that you desire.

As I continue to write about the Power of Your Forgiveness, I am reminded of another story that I read concerning forgiveness many, many years ago. Because it was so long ago, allow me to improvise as I remember it. The story was told by an elementary school teacher who wanted to teach her class the importance of forgiveness. She gave her class a project which consisted of sacks of white potatoes.

Each student was given a sack of potatoes on the first of the month and was told that they had to care for the potatoes as if it were a part of their own bodies for thirty days. They were instructed to take daily notes of their experiences with the potatoes and make a full report after the thirty days was over.

Once the thirty days had passed, each student dragged their sack of potatoes in the class to present their final report. The teacher asked the students what were their findings for the month as they nursed the potatoes? One student said she was doing okay the first few days as she carried the sack, but over time, it became rather heavy and caused her back to hurt. It was hard for her to play games with it while on the playground; therefore, many times she just sat on a bench and watched the kids as they played and enjoyed the game. As the sack grew too heavy for her to carry, she began to drag them everywhere she went, which slowed down her progress. The teacher made a note and moved on to the next student.

The next student said at first, he was excited about the project and was looking forward to caring for the potatoes but after a couple of weeks went by, he noticed that they began to grow extension on them that looked like crooked arms, which scared him. As he tried to break off the extensions, he noticed that they simply grew back in other areas on the potato which seemed like a losing battle, so he just gave up. The teacher made some more notations and moved on to another student.

The next student explained how she experienced similar issues with her sack of potatoes but was rather troubled by her additional findings. She stated that in addition to the potatoes being too heavy to carry, she also was taken aback by the wicked looking appendages that grew uncontrollably, but she noticed something else that was far more disturbing. She said she noticed that after awhile the entire sack of potatoes had a vicious odor. She said, at first it started out with one of the potatoes smelling badly, because it was rotten then the rest of them followed suit. The student realized that since she left the one rotten potato in the sack it spread to the other potatoes, and they too smelled badly because they were now all rotten. The teacher began to smile as she jotted notes on her notepad.

Rather confused, the students wanted to know what the purpose of the project was. The teacher responded that she wanted to show them how necessary forgiveness is to each individual. She explained, when we take offense from someone we take on a burden that is liken to a sack of potatoes.

If you do not forgive an offense quickly, over time the burden will start to weigh heavy on you which can cause you to sit on the sideline and miss out on the game of life. If you do not forgive an offense quickly, after some weeks the burden that you carry can grow extensions, which could be the

If you do not forgive an offense quickly, after some weeks the burden that you carry can grow extensions, which could be the developing of a sickness or disease.

developing of a sickness or disease. Even though you may treat the physical problem with medicine, it may only slow the issue down temporarily but could return in another area of the body because the real cause has yet to be treated. If you do not forgive an offense after awhile your inside will begin to stink because bitterness has now become a resident. This includes your overall attitude, lashing out at others with little cause, your general outlook on life, constant complaining, and always blaming others for your demise are a few symptoms of internal rotting.

As stated above, theorists of the past have asserted that our emotional and mental state has a strong effect on our physical well-being. When we perpetuate negative energy, the affects of these emotions are often displayed through physical issues. It would be to our advantage to cleanse our minds of ill will for anyone, as well as, ourselves to combat this type of phenomenon.

The teacher further explained that she was the one who gave the sack of potatoes to each student and she went home and slept well while the students struggled with the weight, appendages and the smell of the potatoes. This is how offense is given. Once received, the offender goes about their way but the recipient of the offense takes on the burden until it is released through a thought, or an affirmation prayer and/or love. Forgiveness is more for your benefit than it is for the offender. That day the students learned more about forgiveness than most adults care to know.

If you are experiencing some prosperity hesitations, perhaps by asking divine wisdom to reveal to you any issues of offense of which you may need to be made aware. It is vital to be in harmony with yourself and others to solidify the accomplishments of your endeavors. To ignore the need to forgive as a tool would prove to be an unproductive sprint towards your highest good; as the offender will maintain control of YOU through your thoughts.

A woman once asked me, "How do you know that you have forgiven someone?" Quite frankly, if you still want the person(s) dead, that's a good indication that you have not released them. If you want them to suffer, you have not forgiven them, as forgiveness brings peace of mind. When forgiveness is present, you will no longer feel the edge or desire to retaliate when you discover that you have the upper hand in any given situation. Your thoughts of them or the way you start to see them will no longer bother you. I told one man that he will know if he has forgiven when he can compassionately assist his ex-wife if he finds her stranded on the side of a dark deserted road without wanting to see any harm come to her. Or not saying, "That's what you get!" Or, "You deserve that!" There is no need to let ill thoughts prevent the wealth streams from coming to you in great abundance; mentally free your adversary and be at peace!

Forgiveness is an introspective process for the individual who is struggling with harassing thoughts of offense caused by another. It is not mandatory that one should approach a hostile situation or submit to further mistreatment, but it is critical to engage in a personal time of reflecting and cleansing. In this wake, words of forgiveness for others practiced regularly, about 15 to 20 minutes a day, will yield an optimistic conclusion.

When you are upset about something and you are asked, "What are you thinking," but you rather not say, please understand if you don't change any negative thoughts about what has upset you, others will eventually know what you are thinking based on the outcome that manifests for you whether you say it or not. The strong feeling that you have will register in your subconscious mind and will supersede the fact that you said nothing.

Treat your subconscious mind better than you ever have before. Forgive quickly!

I recently read a theory on the subconscious mind that suggested that your conscious mind acts as a male and your subconscious mind as a female. This premise would cause your subconscious mind to hold on to the intensities of every one of your innermost thoughts and how you really feel, and then begin to manifest those feelings in order to give you exactly what you desire! Treat your subconscious mind better than you ever have before. Forgive quickly!

You may utilize the following affirmation to release someone(s) who need your forgiveness. Repeat it as many times as needed until you feel peace: "I forgive you, bless you and loose you from the prison in which I've held you. I wish no hurt or harm for you. I now free you and myself from all debts as I release you in love and peace towards your highest good! Now GO!"

The Power of Your Love

(Sealing the Deal)

As I approached the end of this book I felt things were somewhat off as though I was missing something.

So I reviewed all of my chapters to see if I missed anything, and all of a sudden I knew what it was. I had not covered the most important thing in this world . . . a chapter on Love! Although it's the shortest chapter in the book;

nevertheless, it is the most important emotion on earth and a part of a prosperous life to activate your wealth streams!

The Law of Love is always in order. It is the substance that will pull all of your other efforts together. You cannot accomplish much of anything with optimum success unless you learn to relate to people. Love will absorb a multiplicity of fault that you may see in others and also the mistakes that are found in YOU! It is necessary to start first with YOU and begin to let love radiant through YOU!

Whatever you approach in love, it will eventually return to you multiplied just as you have read about giving. You will quickly notice a difference as you intentionally allow love to shine through you to others.

Take a moment to learn to love YOU! We often struggle with loving others because we don't really love ourselves. We often draw others to us through our past hurts and insecurities while unjustly blaming them as the reason for the non-productive relationship that WE have developed. We hold issues of the past against ourselves and we talk badly about ourselves sometimes on a daily basis, (I'm too fat. I'm too skinny. My lips are too small. My hair is too thin. I'm not smart enough, etc). Realize that there is more to you than your outer appearance. Your inner you is what makes your outer you spectacular. Daily look at yourself in the mirror and say, "I love you!" Therefore, when you decide to first love you, the brilliant light that will shine through you will draw others to you instead of driving them away from you. Love will never fail in any situation that you may find to be difficult.

Not only is love the answer for harmony with your fellowman, it has power to open new wealth streams. As odd as it sounds, no matter what you show love to, it will respond accordingly. So begin to deliberately contemplate love for anything that you want to see flourish in your life. If you want better friends, more money in your wallet, better health, a better home, flourishing business or simply for your car to start when you turn the key, meditate and affirm love towards it by saying: "You have divine love living in you. The Law of Love has already overcome this obstacle, and I am the recipient of a prosperous outcome."

The Power of Your Putting It All Together

(One + One is YOU!)

Okay! Now it's time to put this all together. I can hear you saying and thinking, "This is a lot to do.

How can I organize all of this to do in a day?" Well, I am glad you have asked that question. You have to be honest with yourself to figure out just how badly do you want change? If you can honestly answer that question in the affirmative, then it will be worth the adjustment. Remember, it will work if you apply it but it has to be important enough for you to change by the renewing of your mind. No one can do that for you. So if you are ready, here we go . . .

Just in case you have not started application of these principles already, let me further guide you accordingly. The first thing you will need to do is decide exactly what you want out of life. If it's money, how much is enough? If it's a job/promotion, what type of job do you want? If it's relationship, just what type of relationship do you desire? If it's material things, be as descriptive as you can be for what you decide that you want. This is not as easy as it seems, but once you have decided, the rest should fall into place. This is where your "mind power" and "writing it down" practice will assist with your definitive responses and decisions. It is best not to share your deepest desires with anyone who does not have you in their best interest. This will prove to be dangerous to your dream. Guard your heart's desire with care.

The next phase is equally as important as the first, you must believe that you can and have received it already. Always know whatever you want can belong to you, but you must believe that you can possess it, if not, your efforts will be futile, and the process will stop right here.

Take time to rework your decision until you find that it fits who you are and for what you can believe. If $1,000,000 is hard for you to believe that you can have it then adjust your decision to $100,000 or whatever number your subconscious mind can process for you as believable. Your belief should be one with the rest of your actions, words, and feelings. At this stage, you can start your word affirmations and writings to keep your energy level up and your subconscious aware of what it should be working on for you.

The next step is to see yourself having whatever you decided upon. What does your highest good that you have decided upon look like to you? Imagine scenarios with what you decided on and create events that you can see yourself attending with it. If it's a promotion, what does that look like to you? Can you see your new office? See your name on the door and on a name plate on the desk, visit the section where your employees will be sitting, visualize the Monday meetings, and see your bank statements each Friday with the promotions' increase. See anything that is relevant to that position.

In conjunction with the above, you want to feel and or smell what your new idea would be like once you have it. You should use any of your five senses that you can use to get the feeling that you need to convey to your subconscious that this has happened already and it needs to align with your true feelings.

Please understand that after you have made a decision as to what you desire you can use all of the remaining steps at the same time throughout the day. The main idea is to get an idea and utilize your idea as the bases for your plan. I have listed this process in steps because I am a methodical student and have great respect for that mode of learning. So I understand the need for steps in any process.

As you lay down at night, consciously discuss the idea that you decided to have about yourself with yourself, while seeing it play out in your mind, until you fall to sleep so your subconscious can get to work bringing everything you thought, felt, saw, and spoke into alignment for you. Once you awake, remind yourself of the idea and began to be thankful that you have already received it.

Keep your mind pure, cut off avenues that bring bad news that is critical in nature.

Keep your mind pure, cut off avenues that bring bad news that is critical in nature, drink plenty of water, exercise, continue to babysit your mind with affirmations, and read material that empowers you to excel (like this book)! You can find enhancing audio books to listen to during exercise or while driving. It took you all these years to pollute your thoughts now you will need to apply twice the effort to reprogram and clear your belief system of the junk that you have learned over time. Be persistent, don't be too anxious for anything, it will come; keep your mental energy high. Your outcome all depends on YOU! Now you can see why "Your Prosperity is Your Fault!

AFFIRMATIONS
of
Prosperity

Fears & Worry Affirmations

I cast all of my worries and concerns on the God in me and I am liberated from burdens.

I give thanks that I am no longer worried about lack, for it ran off with fear.

I see myself in profound peace. I rest well every night as my mind manifests sweet dreams and visions.

No fear can withstand my power, love or the strength of my mind. I am free from care.

There is no fear living here. My thoughts are of peace and tranquility. There is hope for tomorrow.

This situation is resolved NOW. I release it to the perfect solution. I let go all doubt and fear now and replace it with power, love and a sound mind.

Financial Affirmations

All of the money that I use returns to me multiplied, in an unlimited cycle of increase and delight.

As I have given away good things I expect to receive good things in great abundance.

Divine rewards come quickly to me for my use. Everything is improving for me financially. My income increases daily.

I do not condemn my bills but give thanks for them as an ideal creation for divine finances. I have all that I need and praise all of my financial associations and interactions NOW.

I am financially prosperous. I am now debt free which is perfect for me.

I direct my mind to think of abundance; my unlimited energy empowers my thinking of sufficiency; my life improves daily; I release all negative attributes from my thoughts; I can no longer accept defeat or limitations; lavish prosperity comes quickly in all that concerns me.

I have the ability to create wealth and the power to be rich without any sorrow. I am an offspring of opulence. I methodically receive prosperity in every phase of my life.

I am prosperous in every area of my life. Only abundance is my portion. I see myself with great wealth.

I live in a world of plenty and I always anticipate plenty. I cannot be limited by anything. My thoughts of prosperity unhinge all limitations.

My income now increases 30, 60 and 100 fold. My mind is now open to wealth.

My maximum good is my nearest good.

My words are ignited with power to create wealth and to circulate money which returns to me multiplied.

Forgiveness Affirmations

I freely forgive all offense received. I am blessed to be happy, full of joy and love.

I forgive you, bless you and loose you from the prison in which I've held you. I wish no hurt or harm for you. I now free you and myself from all debts as I release you in love and peace towards your highest good! Now GO!

I release you from my subconscious mind. All past hurts are cast down and forgiven. I loose you from my thoughts and forgive myself.

I quickly and fully release all who have offended me. I let you go in peace to your elevated good. All is now congenial between us, forever.

Health Affirmations

Divine health radiates in me NOW. Every area of my body is healed, whole and healthy.

Everything related to my health harmoniously works together. My mind, body and spirit are one.

Health reigns supreme in my body. I cannot be ill.

I am healed. I am whole. I am full of light.

I am prospered by my healthy thoughts and positive attitude.

I am thankful for a youthful glow and a radiant countenance. My appearance defies the year I was born.

I see myself living in abundant health. I see myself walking, leaping, and jumping to the tune of wholeness.

I think healthy, eat wise, and heal myself with my thoughts of good ideas of longevity.

My life is full of abundance, health, and peace. I manifest healthy energy inside out.

My mind and body are in perfect shape. Each part glows with joy and energy.

My body is healed NOW. No infirmity, sickness or disease can live within me, so go, NOW!

There is happiness that flows throw my bones, cells, and sinews. All is well with my soul.

There is no illness that can stick to me; health and healing manifest in my daily.

Love Affirmations

Abundance comes quickly when I am harmonious with others. I love eternally.

All of my energy is full of love and joy. I have power to love myself to life, happiness and freedom. I do not condemn anything or anyone. The abundance of love works in me and through me.

I am full of love and light. My great energy is now focused on living my best life. I am thankful for a life that is full love.

There is no negative personality in this Universe. There is only divine love winning in every situation.

My love permeates and transcends through time to reach the depths of all concerned.

You have divine love living in you. The Law of Love has already overcome this obstacle and I am the recipient of a prosperous outcome.

There is no emotion that overpowers me other than love. I choose to love others and others love me. Nothing else can be truer.

Prosperous Life Affirmations

All things work together for my good in order to prosper me.

All that belongs to me by divine right will show up at the right time and comes quickly to me for my use.

As my mind opens to opulence my entire life is destined for greatness.

All of the good that I desire is nearest to me now. My thoughts are filled with opulence and fruitful desires. As I think of good it comes to me multiplied.

I am improving quickly on a daily basis because I am an unlimited resource.

I am a winner, always the victor and more than a conqueror.

I chose to be organized and connected in life. I chose to be successful in every area of my life. I am committed to improving myself at all costs.

I live in the NOW; my daily bread is given.

I must become because I AM.

I release clutter and disorganized thinking. All of my steps are divinely ordered. My focus is clear.

I retain good and prosperous memories. Nothing else can process through my mind. I desire to constantly move forward and never backwards.

I direct my mind to think of abundance; my energy empowers my thinking of sufficiency; my life improves daily.

I release all negative attributes from my thoughts; I can no longer accept defeat or limitations; lavish prosperity comes quickly in all that concerns me NOW.

I expect nothing but the best as I produce excellence as I receive with gratitude and pleasure.

I now let go all negative memories of my past. My positive present now guides me to my optimistic future.

Money is not evil. I choose to use it responsibly for it is the vehicle in which I need to influence change.

My good thoughts of plenty are forever working for me and my inner being creates the life that I desire to live. My eminent good has no limitations. I am free to soar.

My highest good is not limited to my present situation or my past experiences.

My mind is now open to new ideas and witty inventions. I am full of creativity.

Nothing is ever lost. I cannot lose anything that is mine by divine right. It is replaced with its equivalent or something better.

No matter what I see I have the power to change it to what I desire to see.

My God or (the Universe) brings to me all the good that belongs to me in large quantities.

I am in a better place in my life in thirty days as vast improvements come quickly in every area of my life.

Relationship Affirmations

All personalities around me are congenial and kind. I bless all people.

Every person that is designed to be in my world for good is always nearest to me. My steps are divinely ordered as I look for them.

Excellent and immediate results are expected in this situation.

I NOW release unproductive relationships and worn out friendships. I am free from mental manipulation.

My audience is those who respect my worth. No one can prevent my good from coming to me.

Wherever I am peace is always there. I am a magnet for the highest and best relationships.

I appreciate the excellence and finest in everyone. I now draw the most excellent and superlative people to me.

Wealth Quotes

"An investment in knowledge pays the best interest."
Benjamin Franklin

"Fortune sides with him who dares."
Virgil

"Clothes don't make the man. They simply make the man look good."
Dr. I. Franklin Perkins

"The test of our progress is not whether we add more to the abundance of those who have much; it is whether we provide enough for those who have too little."
Franklin D. Roosevelt

"Life does not owe you anything because life has already given you everything."
Ralph Marston

"You can change the course of your life with your words."
Anonymous

"You are already that which you want to be, and your refusal to believe this is the only reason you do not see it."
Neville Goddard

"Words have power, words are power, words could be your power also."Mohammed Qahtani

"Poverty of goods is easily cured; poverty of the mind is irreparable."
Montaigne

"I am not a product of my circumstances. I am a product of my decisions."
Stephen Covey

"Be generous, and someday you will be rewarded."
(CEV) Ecclesiastes 11:1

"The mind is everything. What you think you become."
Buddha

"I always want to become better. If never being satisfied is a problem, then I have it."
King Zlatan Ibrahimovic

"Remember that your real wealth can be measured not by what you have, but by what you are."
Napoleon Hill

"The mouth speaks what the heart is full of."
Anonymous

"The tragedy of life doesn't lie in not reaching your goal. The tragedy lies in having no goal to reach."
Benjamin E. Mayes

"Cry out for insight, and ask for understanding. Search for them as you would for silver; seek them like hidden treasures."
(NLT) Proverbs 2:3-4

"Imagination is everything. It is the preview of life's coming attractions."
Albert Einstein

"I think anything is possible if you have the mindset and the will and desire to do it and put the time in."
Roger Clemens

"The lack of money is the root of all evil."
Mark Twain

"Catch fire today! Make today the day you stop complaining and do something."
Steve Harvey

"Poverty is the parent of revolution and crime."
Aristotle

"Walter Schneider said, "in order to achieve your goals, first you have to have the clarity of what they are."
John Assaraf

"There is gold dust in the air – for you, for me, for everyone."
Catherine Ponder

"Wealth is the ability to fully experience life."
Henry David Thoreau

"You are as you are until you are not."
Jamie Varon

"Economy hasn't changed much we have just become more aware of it."
Dr. I. Franklin Perkins

"Rich people buy luxuries last, while the poor and middle class tend to buy luxuries first."
Robert Kiyosaki

"We become what we think about."
Earl Nightingale

"Rich people have small TVs and big libraries, and poor people have small libraries and big TVs."
Zig Ziglar

"Wealth is largely the result of habit."
John Jacob Astor

"I truly believe in positive synergy, that your positive mindset gives you a more hopeful outlook, and belief that you can do something great means you will do something great."
Russell Wilson

"The person who doesn't know where his next dollar is coming from usually doesn't know where his last dollar went."
Unknown

"We are looking for an apartment; if we do not find anything then we will buy a hotel."
King Zlatan Ibrahimovic

"Your word is your wand."
Florence Scovel Shinn

"Today the greatest single source of wealth is between your ears."
Brian Tracy

"Oh, my friends, if you would just take only four blocks around you, and find out what the people want and what you ought to supply and set them down with your pencil and figure up the profits you would make if you did supply them, you would very soon see it. There is wealth right within the sound of your voice."
Russell Conwell

"That's why they call it the American Dream, because you have to be asleep to believe it."
George Carlin

"Wealth is just consistency . . . I don't want to be rich. I want to be wealthy."
Quavo

"You are the master of your destiny. You can influence, direct and control your own environment. You can make your life what you want it to be."
Napoleon Hill

"You don't have to see the whole staircase. Just take the first step."
Dr. Martin Luther King, Jr.

"Do not withhold good from those to whom it is due, when it is in your power to do it."
(NAS) Proverbs 3:27

"Life is not about finding yourself. Life is about creating yourself."
George Bernard Shaw

"Wealth is in application of mind to nature; and the art of getting rich consists not in industry, much less in saving, but in a better order, in timeliness, in being at the right spot."
Ralph Waldo Emerson

"Give freely and become more wealthy; be stingy and lose everything."
(NLT) Proverbs 11:24

"Poverty is a form of hell caused by man's blindness to God's unlimited good for him. Poverty is a dirty, uncomfortable, degrading experience. Poverty is actually a form of disease, and in its acute phases, it seems to be a form of insanity."
Catherine Ponder

"Logic will get you from A to B. Imagination will take you everywhere."
Albert Einstein

"All you need is time . . . and you have it . . . NOW."
Neville Goddard

"I have a dream . . ."Dr. Martin Luther King

If you would like to book Dr. Perkins for speaking engagements, you may contact her office at:

www.DrIrisPerkins.org

Follow us on:

Twitter	@itsmedrifp
Instagram	@itsmedrifp
Facebook	@itemedrifp

Books may be ordered at:

Amazon.com
BarnesandNoble.com

Other Books Written
by
<u>Dr. I. Franklin Perkins</u>

Deliver Me From . . .

Understanding the Fruit of the Spirit

Equipping Spirit-Led Leaders: Empowering
Current and Potential Leaders for Kingdom
Service

Funeral Foolishness . . . a cry for help!

Your time is NOW!!

CPSIA information can be obtained
at www.ICGtesting.com
Printed in the USA
BVHW04s0501260918
528474BV00016B/73/P